"KNOW YOUR BIBLE
Memory Verse Puzzlers

Written by Gladys Walton

Illustrated by Ann Stein

Cover Illustration by Kathy Marlin
Cover Production by Nehmen-Kodner

All rights reserved—Printed in the U.S.A.
Copyright © 2001 Shining Star Publications
A Division of Frank Schaffer Publications, Inc.
23740 Hawthorne Blvd., Torrance, CA 90505

Table of Contents

SS20024

Introduction

What a great way for children to learn some valuable Bible verses! *"Know Your Bible"* Memory Verse Puzzlers is filled with exciting and inspirational activities that have been designed to help children in grades 2–4 learn all about God's Word, the Bible.

Perfect to use in Sunday school, Christian schools, or at home, the activities featured are fun for children to complete. Children can decode messages, complete word searches, unscramble letters, fill in missing vowels or consonants, do Bible research, and so much more to learn some important messages from the Bible and some valuable Christian principles and concepts.

Each activity features a Bible verse that is relevant and meaningful to the children. Be sure to discuss each Bible verse with them. Encourage the children to memorize these verses and try to live according to the messages they contain. Upon completion of some or all of the activities, reward the children's hard work with a copy of the award on page 64. It is a wonderful way to boost the children's self-esteem.

You will enjoy watching children have fun completing these exciting activities as they grow in God's love!

SS20024

Our Great God

God is the beginning of everything that is or ever has been. He is the Creator of us all. Discover a memory verse about a special beginning by following the directions below very carefully.

| __ | __ | | __ | __ | __ | | __ | __ | __ | __ | __ | __ | __ | __ | __ |
| 1 | 2 | | 3 | 4 | 5 | | 6 | 7 | 8 | 9 | 10 | 11 | 12 | 13 | 14 |

| __ | __ | __ | | __ | __ | __ | __ | __ | __ | __ | | __ | __ | __ |
| 15 | 16 | 17 | | 18 | 19 | 20 | 21 | 22 | 23 | 24 | | 25 | 26 | 27 |

| __ | __ | __ | __ | __ | __ | __ | | __ | __ | __ | | __ | __ | __ |
| 28 | 29 | 30 | 31 | 32 | 33 | 34 | | 35 | 36 | 37 | | 38 | 39 | 40 |

| __ | __ | __ | __ | __ |
| 41 | 42 | 43 | 44 | 45 |

. (Genesis 1:1)

Write an A in blanks 21, 30, 35, 42.

Write a B in blank 6.

Write a C in blank 18.

Write a D in blanks 17, 24, 37.

Write an E in blanks 5, 7, 20, 23, 27, 29, 32, 40, 41.

Write a G in blanks 8, 14, 15.

Write an H in blanks 4, 26, 28, 39, 45.

Write an I in blanks 1, 9, 12.

Write an N in blanks 2, 10, 11, 13, 33, 36.

Write an O in blank 16.

Write an R in blanks 19, 43.

Write an S in blank 34.

Write a T in blanks 3, 22, 25, 38, 44.

Write a V in blank 31.

SS20024

God, the Creator

We know that God was the beginning. He always was and will always be. Use the code below to find something God did. To read the code, go across then down.

Example: 6–C = S

	1	2	3	4	5	6	7	8
A	A	D	G	J	M	P	T	W
B	B	E	H	K	N	R	U	X
C	C	F	I	L	O	S	V	Y

6–C 5–C   3–A 5–C 2–A   1–C 6–B 2–B 1–A 7–A 2–B 2–A

5–A 1–A 5–B   3–C 5–B   3–B 3–C 6–C   5–C 8–A 5–B

3–C 5–A 1–A 3–A 2–B ,   3–C 5–B   7–A 3–B 2–B

3–C 5–A 1–A 3–A 2–B   5–C 2–C   3–A 5–C 2–A

3–B 2–B   1–C 6–B 2–B 1–A 7–A 2–B 2–A   3–B 3–C 5–A ;

5–A 1–A 4–C 2–B   1–A 5–B 2–A   2–C 2–B 5–A 1–A 4–C 2–B

3–B 2–B   1–C 6–B 2–B 1–A 7–A 2–B 2–A   7–A 3–B 2–B 5–A .

(Genesis 1:27)

   SS20024

Honor Your Parents

We are taught from an early age to love and honor our parents. Did you know this is one of God's Ten Commandments? To find out the Bible verse containing this commandment, write the words in numerical order.

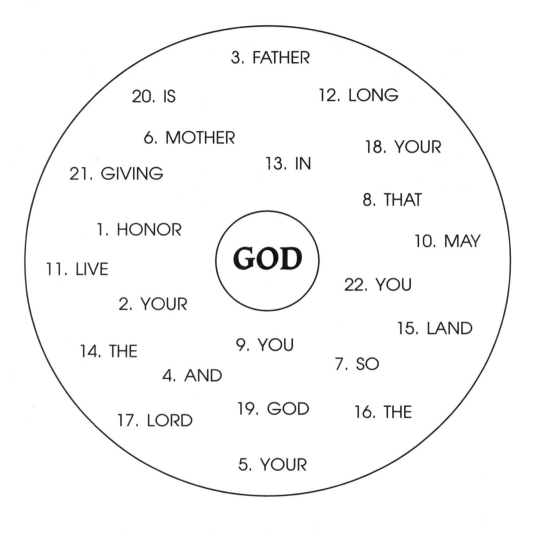

" _____ _____ _____ _____

_____ _____, _____ _____ _____

_____ _____ _____ _____ _____

_____ _____ _____ _____ _____

_____ _____ _____ _____." (Exodus 20:12)

SS20024

Heart of Hearts

The Bible has a lot to say about hearts. Below is a good memory verse for you to learn about YOUR heart. Write the words in the hearts in the right order. The number in each heart tells you how many times the word will be used.

HEART (1)

YOUR (4)

ALL (3)

LORD (1)

LOVE (1)

STRENGTH (1)

AND (2)

WITH (3)

THE (1)

SOUL (1)

GOD (1)

_____ _____ _____ _____ _____

_____ _____ _____ _____ _____

_____ _____ _____ _____ _____

_____ _____ _____ _____ _____ .

(Deuteronomy 6:5)

SS20024

Everlasting Arms

God's love is eternal. He cares for us and holds us up with His everlasting arms. To find a verse relating to this, follow the directions below carefully.

Cross out the color words in lines 1, 3, 8.

Cross out the flower names in lines 6, 10.

Cross out the state names in lines 3, 5, 8.

Cross out the animal names in lines 2, 5, 6, 7, 9, 10.

Cross out the names of the months in lines 2, 5, 10.

Cross out the names of the U.S. presidents in lines 2, 3, 4, 7.

Cross out the names of the parts of the face in lines 1, 4, 7, 8, 9.

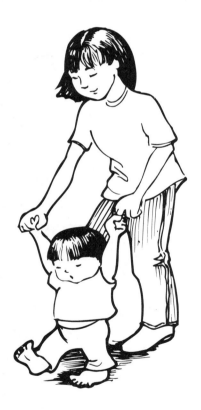

Write the remaining words on the lines below in the order they appear.

1. THEBLUEETERNALEYE
2. MAYGODISTAFTHORSE
3. MONROEYOURREDOHIO
4. REFUGEWILSONCHEEK
5. ARIZONAANDJUNERAT
6. ROSEUNDERNEATHCOW
7. NOSEARECATLINCOLN
8. KANSASGREENTHEEAR
9. LIPSEVERLASTINGDOG
10. PIGIRISARMSAUGUST

"_____ _____ _____ ____ _____

_____, ____ _____ _____

_____ _____ _____ . . ." (Deuteronomy 33:27)

SS20024

God Keeps His Promises

God kept His promises to Joshua. God kept His promises to Moses and Aaron. He will always keep His promises to us as well. To find out how God will keep His promises to you, unscramble the words below and write them on the lines in the correct order.

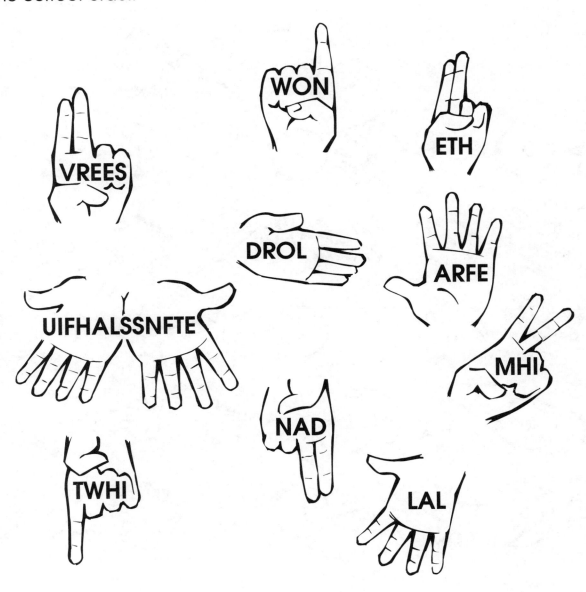

" _____

_____ . . ." (Joshua 24:14)

SS20024

Give Thanks

We have many things to be thankful for. One thing we know is that God's love for us will last forever. We should thank God every day for His love. On the lines below, write down every other letter starting with the first **G**. Then start again with the second **G** and write the remaining letters.

_____ _____ _____ _____ _____ _____,

_____ _____ _____ _____; _____ _____ _____

_____ _____. (1 Chronicles 16:34)

SS20024

Majestic

All you need to do is look around to see how majestic God is. His very name is majestic! Use the code to find out more about this.

Tip: To help you remember this verse, repeat it once every day.

A	B	C	D	E	F	G	H	I	J	K	L	M
N	O	P	Q	R	S	T	U	V	W	X	Y	Z

_____ , _____ _____, _____ _____ _____ _____

_____ _____ _____ _____

_____ _____ _____ _____ _____ _____ _____ ! . . . (Psalm 8:1)

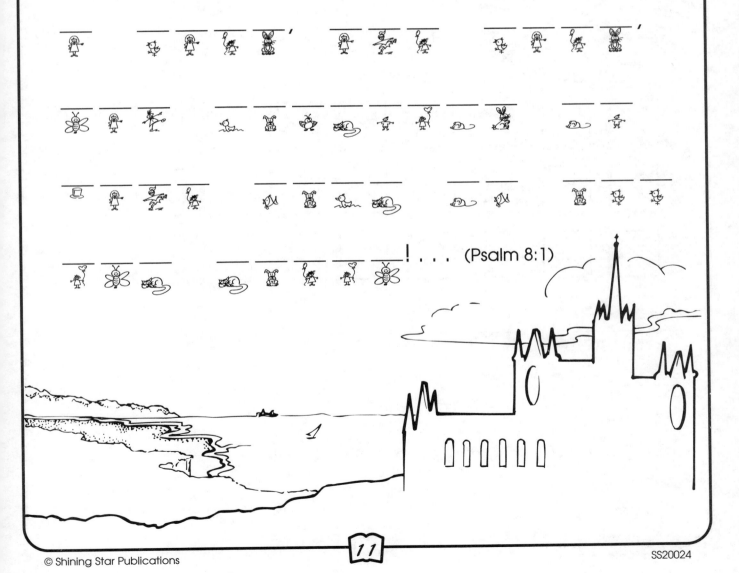

SS20024

Joyous Heart

Loving the Lord brings joy to one's heart. The verse below is a good one to learn to remember this. Decode the verse by using the code. Write the letters above the corresponding numbers.

Example: 1 = A

A / 1	B / 2	C / 3	D / 4	E / 5	F / 6	G / 7	H / 8	I / 9
J / 10	K / 11	L / 12	M / 13	N / 14	O / 15	P / 16	Q / 17	R / 18
S / 19	T / 20	U / 21	V / 22	W / 23	X / 24	Y / 25	Z / 26	

20 8 5   16 18 5 3 5 16 20 19   15 6

20 8 5   12 15 18 4   1 18 5

18 9 7 8 20 ,   7 9 22 9 14 7   10 15 25

20 15   20 8 5   8 5 1 18 20 . . .   (Psalm 19:8)

SS20024

Days of Our Lives

God's love goes with us wherever we go. He is our guide. Write down the letters in the odd numbered columns starting with **S**, and going across each row. (The first two have been done for you.) Then go back and write all the letters in the even numbered columns starting with **M**.

1	2	3	4	5	6	7	8	9	10	11	12
S	M	U	Y	R	L	E	I	L	F	Y	E
G	A	O	N	O	D	D	I	N	W	E	I
S	L	S	L	A	D	N	W	D	E	L	L
O	L	V	I	E	N	W	T	I	H	L	E
L	H	F	O	O	U	L	S	L	E	O	O
W	F	M	T	E	H	A	E	L	L	L	O
T	R	H	D	E	F	D	O	A	R	Y	E
S	V	O	E	F	R						

Su _____

_____

_____

_____

_____

_____

_____

_____

(Psalm 23:6)

SS20024

All the Earth

God owns the whole earth and all that is in it. Break the code to find a verse in the book of Psalms to learn more about everything God owns.

1 = A	2 = B	3 = D
4 = E	5 = F	6 = G
7 = H	8 = I	9 = L
10 = N	11 = O	12 = P
13 = R	14 = S	15 = T
16 = U	17 = V	18 = W
	19 = Y	

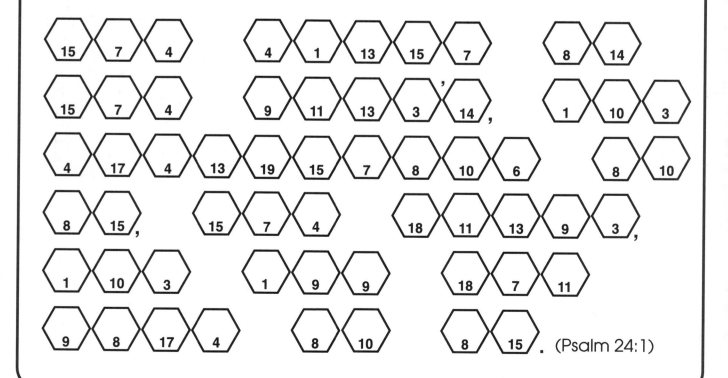

15 7 4   4 1 13 15 7   8 14

15 7 4   9 11 13 3 14,   1 10 3

4 17 4 13 19 15 7 8 10 6   8 10

8 15,   15 7 4   18 11 13 9 3,

1 10 3   1 9 9   18 7 11

9 8 17 4   8 10   8 15. (Psalm 24:1)

SS20024

A New Heart

If you open your Bible to the very center, you will probably see the book of Psalms. This book is one of the best. A great Bible verse for you to learn from this book is scrambled in the heart below. See if you can write it correctly under the heart. The first word has been done for you.

STEADFAST
IN
AND
SPIRIT
ME
HEART
GOD
O
A
ME
PURE
WITHIN
RENEW
A

CREATE _____

_____

_____

(Psalm 51:10)

SS20024

Rejoice in His Name

Do you get excited and want to rejoice sometimes? We all like to rejoice when we are happy. One of the best ways to rejoice is to rejoice in the Lord. Write every other letter in the odd rows starting with the **T**. Then go back and write down all the letters left in the even rows starting with the **H**.

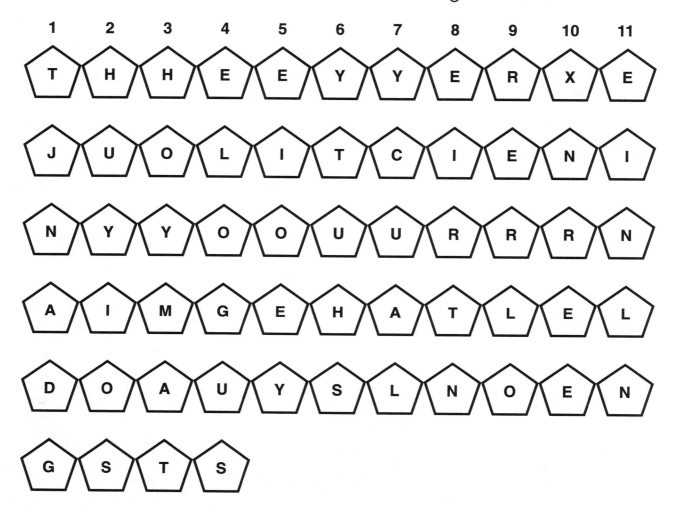

1	2	3	4	5	6	7	8	9	10	11
T	H	H	E	E	Y	Y	E	R	X	E
J	U	O	L	I	T	C	I	E	N	I
N	Y	Y	O	O	U	U	R	R	R	N
A	I	M	G	E	H	A	T	L	E	L
D	O	A	U	Y	S	L	N	O	E	N
G	S	T	S							

Write the verse.

_____

_____

_____

_____ (Psalm 89:16)

SS20024

Abounding in Love

God's love abounds forever. His love for us is unconditional. Use the math code to find out about His love for us.

A = 1	I = 9	Q = 17
B = 2	J = 10	R = 18
C = 3	K = 11	S = 19
D = 4	L = 12	T = 20
E = 5	M = 13	U = 21
F = 6	N = 14	V = 22
G = 7	O = 15	W = 23
H = 8	P = 16	Y = 24

$\overline{19+1}$ $\overline{4+4}$ $\overline{12-7}$ $\overline{20-8}$ $\overline{7+8}$ $\overline{9+9}$ $\overline{9-5}$ $\overline{10-1}$ $\overline{15+4}$

$\overline{11-8}$ $\overline{7+8}$ $\overline{6+7}$ $\overline{8+8}$ $\overline{10-9}$ $\overline{15+4}$ $\overline{15+4}$ $\overline{10-1}$ $\overline{7+8}$ $\overline{7+7}$ $\overline{10-9}$ $\overline{19+1}$ $\overline{12-7}$

$\overline{10-9}$ $\overline{7+7}$ $\overline{9-5}$ $\overline{15-8}$ $\overline{9+9}$ $\overline{10-9}$ $\overline{11-8}$ $\overline{10-1}$ $\overline{7+8}$ $\overline{24-3}$ $\overline{15+4}$,

$\overline{15+4}$ $\overline{20-8}$ $\overline{7+8}$ $\overline{24-1}$ $\overline{19+1}$ $\overline{7+8}$ $\overline{10-9}$ $\overline{7+7}$ $\overline{15-8}$ $\overline{12-7}$ $\overline{9+9}$,

$\overline{10-9}$ $\overline{10-8}$ $\overline{7+8}$ $\overline{24-3}$ $\overline{7+7}$ $\overline{9-5}$ $\overline{10-1}$ $\overline{7+7}$ $\overline{15-8}$ $\overline{10-1}$ $\overline{7+7}$

$\overline{20-8}$ $\overline{7+8}$ $\overline{20+2}$ $\overline{12-7}$ _____ . (Psalm 103:8)

SS20024

I Will Rejoice!

Every day is the day to rejoice in the Lord. He made a beautiful world for us to enjoy. Use the code below to discover a verse about rejoicing.

1 = H	12 = Q	23 = G
2 = O	13 = C	24 = S
3 = R	14 = I	25 = N
4 = U	15 = L	26 = F
5 = K	16 = T	
6 = Y	17 = B	
7 = W	18 = V	
8 = J	19 = M	
9 = E	20 = A	
10 = P	21 = X	
11 = D	22 = Z	

‾‾ ‾‾ ‾‾ ‾‾   ‾‾ ‾‾   ‾‾ ‾‾ ‾‾   ‾‾ ‾‾ ‾‾
16 1 14 24   14 24   16 1 9   11 20 6

‾‾ ‾‾ ‾‾   ‾‾ ‾‾ ‾‾ ‾‾   ‾‾ ‾‾ ‾‾
16 1 9   15 2 3 11   1 20 24

‾‾ ‾‾ ‾‾ ‾‾ ;   ‾‾ ‾‾ ‾‾   ‾‾ ‾‾
19 20 11 9   15 9 16   4 24

‾‾ ‾‾ ‾‾ ‾‾ ‾‾ ‾‾ ‾‾   ‾‾ ‾‾ ‾‾   ‾‾ ‾‾
 3 9 8 2 14 13 9   20 25 11   17 9

‾‾ ‾‾ ‾‾ ‾‾   ‾‾ ‾‾   ‾‾ ‾‾ . (Psalm 118:24)
23 15 20 11   14 25   14 16

18

SS20024

Hide It in Your Heart

The Bible tells us to love God. In order to do that, we must learn His Word. We need to memorize it over and over so that we will hide it deep in our hearts.

Find the words in the word search below, looking up, down, forward, backward, and diagonally. Then write the verse on the lines below.

```
P  R  L  T  H  A  T  I  M  L  O  J
H  E  A  R  T  H  H  X  Y  J  J  S
O  S  C  W  I  Y  O  U  A  I  Y  Z
N  B  I  H  A  V  E  O  Z  O  H  R
E  N  W  A  G  A  I  N  S  T  K  X
H  I  O  M  L  H  I  D  D  E  N  F
U  N  R  L  K  I  V  M  E  S  G  R
N  E  D  A  Z  Q  F  I  I  I  G  U
D  T  S  S  X  U  M  N  G  G  U  O
R  E  U  P  A  N  X  M  L  T  H  Y
E  E  P  P  O  I  V  Y  V  M  V  T
D  N  X  T  J  E  L  E  V  E  N  K
```

I HAVE	IN MY	NOT	PSALM
HIDDEN	HEART	SIN	ONE HUNDRED
YOUR	THAT I	AGAINST	NINETEEN
WORD	MIGHT	YOU	ELEVEN

_____

_____

_____

SS20024

God's Word Is a Lamp

God's Word is a lamp to us. It lights the way before us. All we need to do is follow it. Decode the memory verse below using the keypad. The first number tells you which key to look at; the second tells you which letter to write.

Example: 4–2 = H

$\underset{9-3}{\rule{1cm}{0.4pt}}$ $\underset{6-3}{\rule{1cm}{0.4pt}}$ $\underset{8-2}{\rule{1cm}{0.4pt}}$ $\underset{7-2}{\rule{1cm}{0.4pt}}$ $\underset{9-1}{\rule{1cm}{0.4pt}}$ $\underset{6-3}{\rule{1cm}{0.4pt}}$ $\underset{7-2}{\rule{1cm}{0.4pt}}$ $\underset{3-1}{\rule{1cm}{0.4pt}}$ $\underset{4-3}{\rule{1cm}{0.4pt}}$ $\underset{7-3}{\rule{1cm}{0.4pt}}$ $\underset{2-1}{\rule{1cm}{0.4pt}}$

9–3 6–3 8–2 7–2   9–1 6–3 7–2 3–1   4–3 7–3   2–1

5–3 2–1 6–1 7–1   8–1 6–3   6–1 9–3   3–3 3–2 3–2 8–1

2–1 6–2 3–1   2–1   5–3 4–3 4–1 4–2 8–1   3–3 6–3 7–2

6–1 9–3   7–1 2–1 8–1 4–2 . (Psalm 119:105)

SS20024

Praise

People praise God in different ways. Some sing, and some praise Him with their speech. We can praise Him, too. Use the code below to find an important reason to praise God.

A	B	C	D	E	F	G	H	I	J	K	L	M
✿	◉	✔	❄	♥	✦	🌿	★	✖	✪	❀	✝	✚

N	O	P	Q	R	S	T	U	V	W	X	Y	Z
■	●	▢	✳	☆	▲	▼	◆	❖	◗	✺	◗	❣

_____

_____

_____

_____. (Psalm 146:10)

Write some things you praise God for.

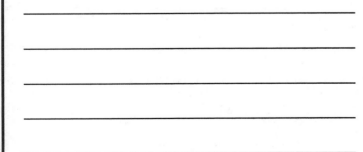

_____

_____

_____

_____

_____

SS20024

Your Understanding

We must trust in the Lord if we want His help. On the lines below, write the first word in section 1, continuing through section 4. Write the second word in section 2 and keep going until all words in each section have been written.

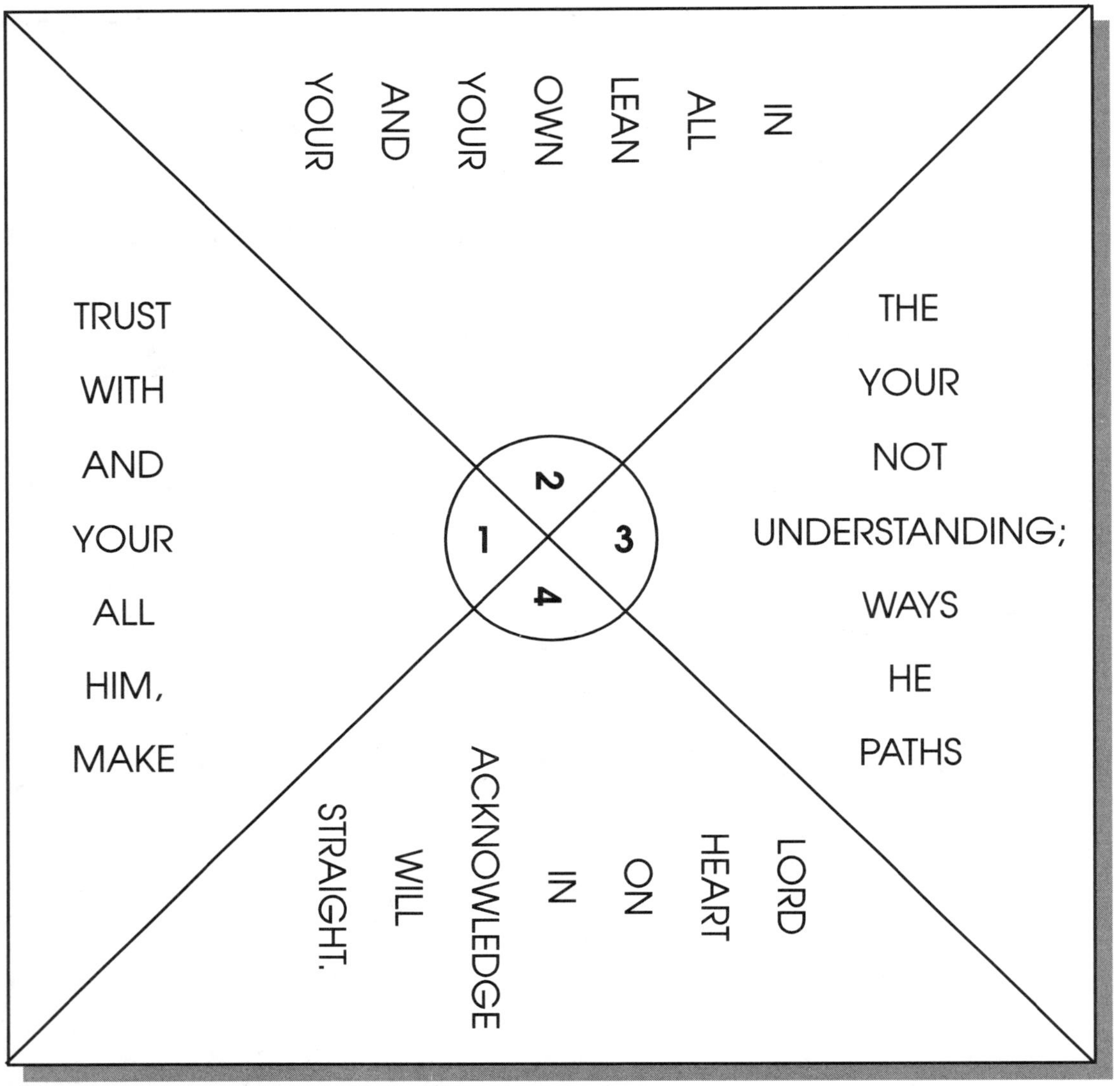
1
TRUST
WITH
AND
YOUR
ALL
HIM,
MAKE
2
IN
ALL
LEAN
OWN
YOUR
AND
YOUR
3
THE
YOUR
NOT
UNDERSTANDING;
WAYS
HE
PATHS
4
LORD
HEART
ON
IN
ACKNOWLEDGE
WILL
STRAIGHT.

____

____

____

____

(Proverbs 3:5–6)

God's Glory

God's glory is everywhere. All we have to do is look around, and we can appreciate His glory. Use the code below to find out about God's glory. Then write the Bible verse on a card and carry it with you.

A = 1 F = 4 I = 7 M = 10 R = 13 U = 16 Y = 19

D = 2 G = 5 K = 8 N = 11 S = 14 V = 17

E = 3 H = 6 L = 9 O = 12 T = 15 W = 18

. . . "H O L Y , H O L Y , H O L Y
       6 12 9 19   6 12 9 19   6 12 9 19

I S   T H E   L O R D
7 14   15 6 3   9 12 13 2

A L M I G H T Y ; T H E
1 9 10 7 5 6 15 19 15 6 3

W H O L E   E A R T H   I S
18 6 12 9 3 3 1 13 15 6 7 14

F U L L   O F   H I S
4 16 9 9   12 4   6 7 14

G L O R Y ." (Isaiah 6:3)
5 9 12 13 19

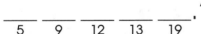

SS20024

Trust in the Lord

Did you ever have a friend you could trust with anything? Jesus is just such a friend. He will help you, but first, you must learn to trust Him. Use the code to find a verse about trust.

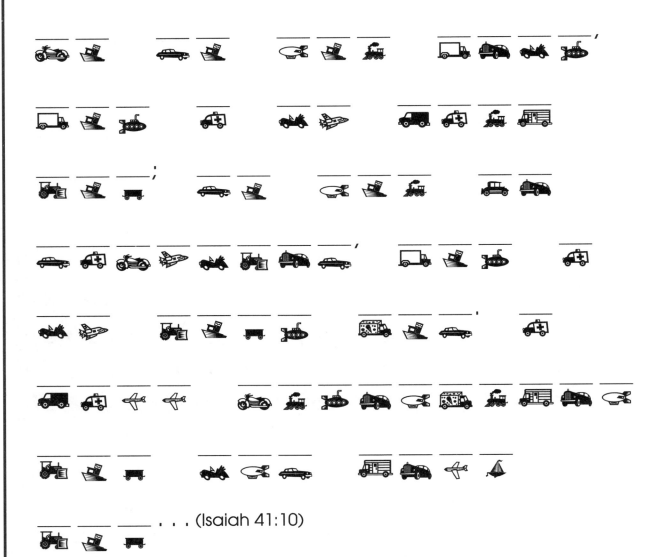

SS20024

Heart's Delight

You have probably heard people talk about their "heart's delight." Did you wonder what they meant? This saying means different things to different people. Look up Jeremiah 15:16. Then start at the upper left corner and go through the maze to find the hidden words to finish the verse below. Do not go diagonally, only down or across.

```
Y  O  C  J  P  M  Q  L  V  C  R  S  T  P  A  S  M
L  U  M  T  R  Y  U  I  V  R  A  G  C  O  E  P  L
S  R  W  O  L  N  J  C  Z  T  P  L  N  R  C  E  K
J  E  D  R  T  V  C  D  N  M  L  P  K  N  I  S  G
A  C  P  D  S  L  I  J  K  M  Y  T  O  R  Q  T  F
H  P  C  E  W  O  M  N  H  I  S  T  R  N  G  E  L
R  C  E  P  E  R  E  S  T  M  K  L  N  B  R  S  P
M  Z  Q  E  R  C  M  L  V  W  C  G  P  E  R  F  T
N  S  C  A  Q  T  Y  J  O  R  F  G  I  C  E  M  I
C  Y  B  N  I  T  C  H  Y  A  F  D  C  P  R  M  O
W  R  T  U  C  P  R  N  T  N  X  C  P  I  U  Y  L
H  P  C  R  I  Q  T  E  R  D  M  Y  E  C  R  O  E
J  P  C  R  M  N  I  T  Y  A  F  H  C  N  A  E  R
H  B  I  L  R  E  F  N  F  T  G  E  R  A  T  C  I
Q  P  C  C  B  I  N  O  E  R  T  A  R  T  Z  N  Y
H  N  I  P  L  N  T  U  R  E  S  I  O  S  X  Y  A
S  P  C  A  L  M  J  Y  T  E  R  D  C  D  A  V  C
C  R  G  H  P  N  I  J  B  H  V  B  C  E  L  I  H
J  N  M  Y  T  R  F  C  E  D  S  Y  F  G  M  G  H
J  N  O  P  L  I  M  N  Y  U  R  C  T  I  R  K  T
```

When _____ _____ *came, I ate them; they* _____

_____ _____ _____ _____ _____ _____

_____ . . . *(Jeremiah 15:16)*

SS20024

God Loves You

Do you know that God loves you? His love for you is unconditional. He has always loved you. God wants what is best for you. Cross out every B, C, and X to find out how much you are loved. Write the remaining letters as they appear on the lines below.

BIBC   XHCCABVXE   XCLBOCXVXEBCD   XYCBOCU
CXWBCIXTH   CAXBNB   CEVXEXRCLBABSCBXTCIXNG
CLXBOCVXBCE   XBIC   XCBBCHBXACXBVCXXE
CDXBRXCABWXCBN   BCXYCXOCBU   BWCIXTCXH
XBLCOXBVCXICBNXCBG–BKCXIBNXDCBNXEBSCS

. . . "— ——— ———— ———

———— —— ——————————

———; —— ————— ———

——— ———— —————-

—— —— —— ——." (Jeremiah 31:3)

Our Refuge

God is our refuge. He is our shelter. We can escape to Him with our problems, and He is always there for us. Cross out one letter in each word below to find a verse about God being our refuge.

Tip: Write the verse on a small card and carry it with you. Repeat it often.

_____ _____ _____ _____, _____
THES   ALORD   TIS   GOLOD   NA

_____ _____ _____ _____
RETFUGE   TIN   TRIMES   SOF

_____. _____ _____ _____
TRAOUBLE   SHE   SCARES   FEOR

_____ _____ _____ ____ _____.
THEOSE   WEHO   TRHUST   TIN   HTIM

(Nahum 1:7)

SS20024

Immanuel

God promised that He would be with us at all times. He promised to send His Son into the world to save His people from their sins. They called God's Son Immanuel because it means, "God with us." Add the missing vowels to learn the verse found in Matthew 1:23. Then write in the verse on the lines at the bottom of the page.

"TH__   V__RG__N   W__LL   B__   W__TH   CH__LD   __ND

W__LL   G__VE   B__RTH   T__   __   S__N,   __ND   TH__Y

W__LL   C__LL   H__M   __MM__N__ __L" — WH__CH

M__ __NS,   "G__D   W__TH   __S." (Matthew 1:23)

_____

_____

_____

_____

SS20024

Fishers of Men

Many people like to fish. Others don't care to fish, but they like to eat fish. Still others have fish for pets. No matter what you like, Jesus told us something about fishing. Unscramble each word on the fish below. Then write the verse correctly on the lines.

MEOC

LLOFOW

EM

"_____, _____ _____"

SEUSJ

SADI

NDA

_____ _____, "_____

I

LWLI

KEAM

OUY

_____ _____ _____ _____

SIHFRES

FO

EMN

_____ _____ _____."

(Matthew 4:19)

SS20024

Pure in Heart

The Bible contains many great things. Among them are some exact words that Jesus spoke. One of the great things Jesus said is found in the book of Matthew. Use the code below to learn this verse.

1 = A	10 = N
2 = B	11 = O
3 = D	12 = P
4 = E	13 = R
5 = F	14 = S
6 = G	15 = T
7 = H	16 = U
8 = I	17 = W
9 = L	18 = Y

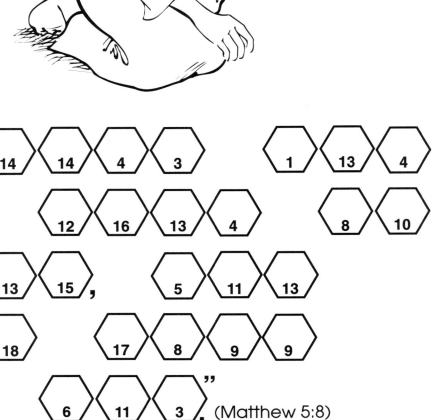

" 2 9 4 14 14 4 3   1 13 4

15 7 4   12 16 13 4   8 10

7 4 1 13 15 ,   5 11 13

15 7 4 18   17 8 9 9

14 4 4   6 11 3 . "   (Matthew 5:8)

SS20024

Let Your Light Shine

What does it mean to let your light shine? Jesus tells us to let our lights shine before men. Use a mirror to read the verse below. Then see if you can write it without looking. Practice doing this until you can do it perfectly.

"IN THE SAME WAY, LET
YOUR LIGHT SHINE
BEFORE MEN, THAT THEY
MAY SEE YOUR GOOD
DEEDS AND PRAISE YOUR
FATHER IN HEAVEN."
(MATTHEW 5:16)

_____

_____

_____ (Matthew 5:16)

   SS20024

Love Your Enemies

Jesus loves everyone, no matter what color they are. He even loves the people who nailed Him to the cross. Find the words from the Bible verse in the word search. Look up, down, forward, backward, and diagonally. Then write the verse.

```
Y  X  E  N  Z  K  E  T  K  I  D  G
O  C  V  P  U  E  T  F  W  W  P  S
U  E  I  N  S  R  U  O  Q  E  V  J
R  E  F  O  V  F  C  R  K  H  Z  R
E  V  H  V  K  D  E  T  E  T  R  R
Y  T  O  H  V  N  S  Y  N  T  J  Y
J  S  O  H  W  A  R  F  E  A  P  N
H  J  H  P  W  Y  E  O  M  M  T  V
L  T  W  Y  X  H  P  U  I  A  O  Y
L  O  V  E  A  R  D  R  E  K  O  J
F  F  O  R  K  R  B  M  S  U  O  K
P  W  F  W  Q  J  P  D  L  N  S  R
```

LOVE	AND	THOSE	YOU	FORTY-FOUR
YOUR	PRAY	WHO	MATTHEW	
ENEMIES	FOR	PERSECUTE	FIVE	

".. . _____

_____

_____. " _____

SS20024

Ask and Receive

When you ask your mom or dad for something, you probably expect them to give it to you. When we ask God for something, He will give it to us or do it for us if we believe He will. Use the code to find out what God will do for us.

Tip: An easy way for you to remember this verse is with three simple words.

Ask
Seek
Knock

A	B	C	D	E	F	G	H	I	J	K	L	M
📁	📄	✂	✍	✏	⏳	☝	〰	✋	☺	🔔	●	❄

N	O	P	Q	R	S	T	U	V	W	X	Y	Z
■	□	⚑	✈	☀	🌢	◆	◆	❖	◆	📖	✉	☎

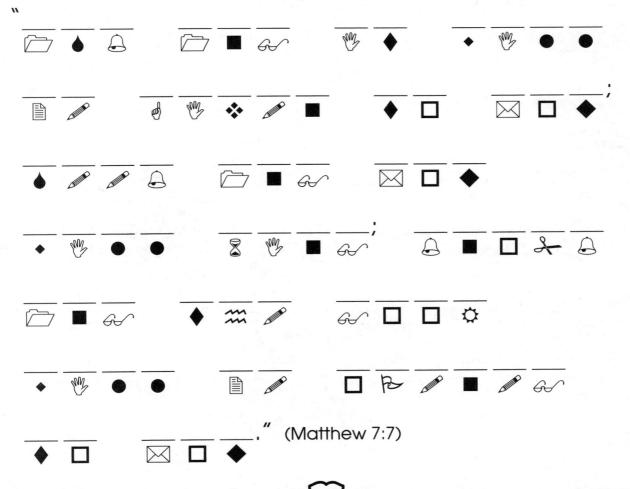

"_____ _____ _____ _____ _____ _____ _____ _____ _____ _____ _____ _____

_____ _____ _____ _____ _____ _____ _____ _____ _____ _____ _____ _____ ;

_____ _____ _____ _____ _____ _____ _____ _____ _____ _____

_____ _____ _____ _____ _____ _____ _____ _____ ; _____ _____ _____ _____ _____

_____ _____ _____ _____ _____ _____ _____ _____ _____ _____

_____ _____ _____ _____ _____ _____ _____ _____ _____ _____ _____ _____

_____ _____ _____ _____ _____ _____ ." (Matthew 7:7)

SS20024

Faith

The Bible has much to say about faith. We have faith in many things, but God wants our faith to be in Him. Each word below has one extra letter in it. Cross out the extra letter and write the word on the line above it.

Tip: Write the verse on a 3" x 5" card. Put it on your mirror. Repeat the verse every day until you can say it without help.

_____ _____ _____ _____
TSHEN   THE   TOOUCHED   THEIRE

_____ _____ _____, "_____
TEYES   SAND   SLAID   ACCOARDING

_____ _____ _____ _____ _____
TON   SYOUR   FIAITH   SWILL   PIT

_____ _____ _____ _____." (Matthew 9:29)
SBE   DRONE   TOY   YOUR

SS20024

A Message

John the Baptist went about telling people of the Savior who was coming to save people from sin. John went ahead to prepare the way for Jesus. To find out what message John was telling the people, cross out every other letter below starting with **T**. Write the remaining letters on the lines below.

TAHNLDC   TPHAIRS   OWIABSE   HTICS

PMIELSFSDARGCEK   AVFWTXETR   HMAE

MWAITLEL   DCVOKMXE   HOLNVE   CMAOBRVE

DPTOAWLEBRCFMUIL   ATOHCATN   RI   MTCHRE

STLHIOANNGAS   MOIF   JWAHIOMSIE

PSTAONCDKARLIS   TIL   AGM   VNEORTI

WAOJRCTPHAY   DTWO   CSITBOEOMP

JDSOTWIN   LAANRD   DULNCTZIME.

___ ___ ____ ____ ____

___ ___ _____:

" _____ __ ____

__ ____ ___ ____

___ ___ ____ ____

__, ___ ____ ____

__ __ ___ _____

___ __ ____ _____

___ _____ ." (Mark 1:7)

SS20024

The Little Children

Jesus loves everyone, especially little children. The Bible tells us we must become as little children in order to enter the kingdom of heaven. Fit the words from the verse below into the puzzle.

"Whoever welcomes one of these little children in my name welcomes me . . ."

W E L C O M E S

Write the verse here.

_____

_____

_____ (Mark 9:37)

SS20024

Rich but Poor

A rich young ruler came to ask of Jesus what he must do to have eternal life. Jesus told him he must keep the commandments and sell what he had and give it to the poor. To find out why Jesus told him this, write the verse below in the correct order on the lines.

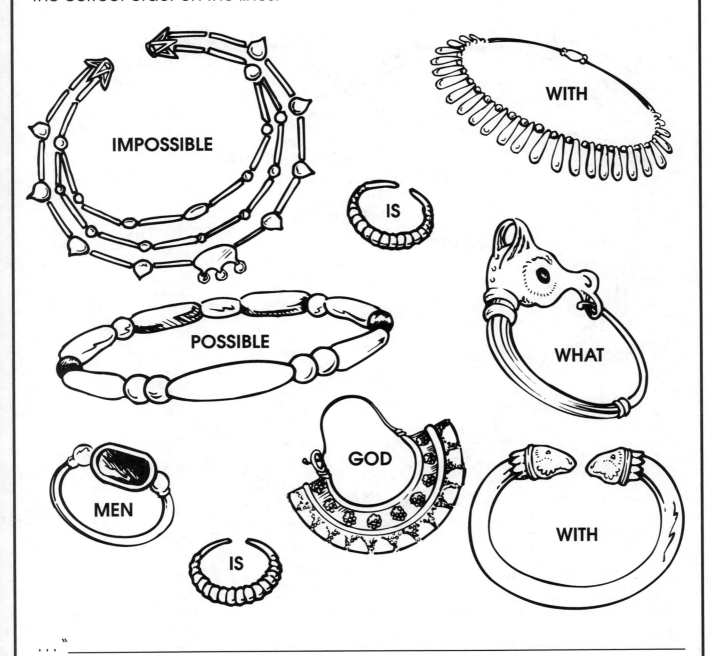

. . . " _____

_____." (Luke 18:27)

SS20024

Eternal Life

From a very early age, we hear about how much God loves us. He even sent His Son to die for us! The heart below has a verse about God's love for us. Write the verse in the correct order on the lines.

SON   HIS

HE   SO   ONLY

GOD   THAT   LIFE

WHOEVER   AND

ONE   BELIEVES   THE

LOVED   HIM

WORLD   IN

THAT   PERISH

SHALL

NOT   GAVE

BUT   ETERNAL

FOR

HAVE

" _____

_____

_____." (John 3:16)

SS20024

Jesus Is the Way

Jesus gave His disciples instructions on how to live. He told them to live for Him and obey His Word. Decode the verse to find an important message.

A	B	C	D	E	F	G	H	I	J	K	L	M
N	O	P	Q	R	S	T	U	V	W	X	Y	Z

"

   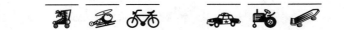 

_____ ___." (John 14:6)

SS20024

Salvation

The Bible tells us that we need to believe God. We must trust Him to be our salvation. Use the code to write the verse below. (Example: 4–B = K)

	1	2	3	4	5	6	7	8
A	A	D	G	J	M	P	T	W
B	B	E	H	K	N	R	U	X
C	C	F	I	L	O	S	V	Y

___ ___ ___   ___ ___ ___ ___ ___ ___ ___ ___
1–A 5–B 2–A   2–B 7–C 2–B 6–B 8–C 5–C 5–B 2–B

___ ___ ___   ___ ___ ___ ___ ___   ___ ___   ___ ___ ___
8–A 3–B 5–C   1–C 1–A 4–C 4–C 6–C   5–C 5–B   7–A 3–B 2–B

___ ___ ___ ___   ___ ___   ___ ___ ___   ___ ___ ___ ___
5–B 1–A 5–A 2–B   5–C 2–C   7–A 3–B 2–B   4–C 5–C 6–B 2–A

___ ___ ___ ___   ___ ___   ___ ___ ___ ___ ___.' " (Acts 2:21)
8–A 3–C 4–C 4–C   1–B 2–B   6–C 1–A 7–C 2–B 2–A

SS20024

Believe

All people must choose for themselves what they believe in. No one forces us to believe in God. We need only look around to see the handiwork of God everywhere. To learn an important verse about believing, write the words in numerical order.

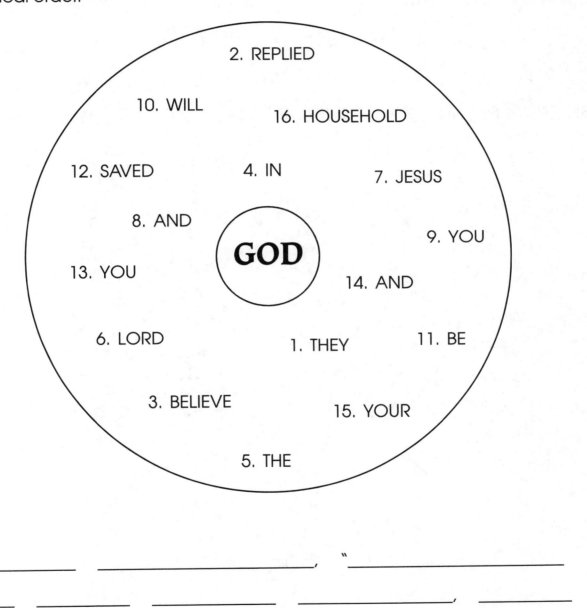

2. REPLIED

10. WILL

16. HOUSEHOLD

12. SAVED

4. IN

7. JESUS

8. AND

GOD

9. YOU

13. YOU

14. AND

6. LORD

1. THEY

11. BE

3. BELIEVE

15. YOUR

5. THE

_____ _____ _____, "_____

_____ _____ _____ _____, _____

_____ _____ _____ _____ —

_____ _____ _____ _____ ." (Acts 16:31)

SS20024

Christ Died for Us

In the verse below, all the vowels have been omitted. Write the correct vowel in each blank. Then write the verse on the lines below.

Tip: When learning a verse, say the reference, then the verse. Then repeat the reference once more.

B__T   G__D   D__M__NSTR__T__S   H__S   __WN   L__V__

F__R   __S   __N   TH__S: WH__L__   W__   W__R__

ST__LL   S__NN__RS,   CHR__ST   D__ __D   F__R   __S.

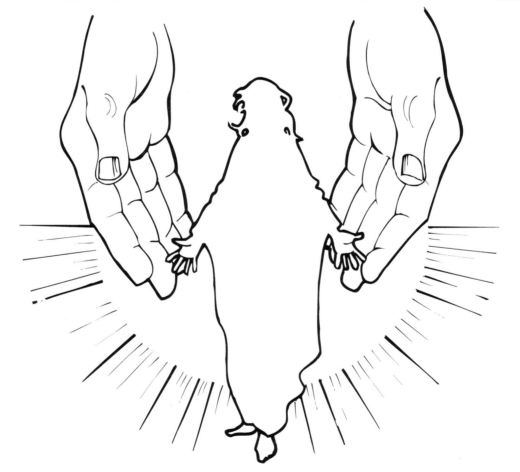

_____

_____

_____ (Romans 5:8)

SS20024

God's Gift for You

God sent His Son into the world to die for our sins. He did this because His love for us is so great. When Jesus died for us, it was so we could receive a gift from God. Use the math code to find out what this gift is.

A = 1   D = 4   G = 7   J = 10   M = 13   P = 16   S = 19   V = 22   Y = 25

B = 2   E = 5   H = 8   K = 11   N = 14   Q = 17   T = 20   W = 23   Z = 26

C = 3   F = 6   I = 9   L = 12   O = 15   R = 18   U = 21   X = 24

$\overline{3+3}$ $\overline{16-1}$ $\overline{9+9}$ $\overline{19+1}$ $\overline{12-4}$ $\overline{4+1}$

$\overline{22+1}$ $\overline{10-9}$ $\overline{3+4}$ $\overline{4+1}$ $\overline{18+1}$ $\overline{16-1}$ $\overline{3+3}$ $\overline{18+1}$ $\overline{4+5}$ $\overline{7+7}$

$\overline{4+5}$ $\overline{18+1}$ $\overline{9-5}$ $\overline{4+1}$ $\overline{10-9}$ $\overline{19+1}$ $\overline{12-4}$' $\overline{1+1}$ $\overline{23-2}$ $\overline{19+1}$

$\overline{19+1}$ $\overline{12-4}$ $\overline{4+1}$ $\overline{3+4}$ $\overline{4+5}$ $\overline{3+3}$ $\overline{19+1}$ $\overline{16-1}$ $\overline{3+3}$

$\overline{3+4}$ $\overline{16-1}$ $\overline{9-5}$ $\overline{4+5}$ $\overline{18+1}$

$\overline{4+1}$ $\overline{19+1}$ $\overline{4+1}$ $\overline{9+9}$ $\overline{7+7}$ $\overline{10-9}$ $\overline{6+6}$

$\overline{6+6}$ $\overline{4+5}$ $\overline{3+3}$ $\overline{4+1}$ $\overline{4+5}$ $\overline{7+7}$

$\overline{5-2}$ $\overline{6+2}$ $\overline{9+9}$ $\overline{5+4}$ $\overline{22-3}$ $\overline{8+12}$

$\overline{5+5}$ $\overline{4+1}$ $\overline{18+1}$ $\overline{23-2}$ $\overline{18+1}$ $\overline{16-1}$ $\overline{23-2}$ $\overline{9+9}$

$\overline{6+6}$ $\overline{16-1}$ $\overline{9+9}$ $\overline{9-5}$. (Romans 6:23)

SS20024

God's Love Is Forever

God is always doing things for our good. He loves us and will do things for our good. Some of the letters in the memory verse below have been replaced by others. Use the code to learn the verse. (Example: O = N)

Change all the O's to N's.
Change all the A's to T's.
Change all the X's to H's.
Change all the Q's to I's.
Change all the P's to S's.
Change all the Z's to A's.
Change all the N's to O's.
Change all the T's to L's.
Change all the C's to E's.
Change all the L's to G's.
Change all the S's to R's.
Change all the B's to W's.

Keep the rest of the letters the same.

Z O D   B C   K O N B   A X Z A

Q O   Z T T   A X Q O L P   L N D

B N S K P   F N S   A X C

L N N D   N F   A X N P C   B X N

T N V C   X Q M . . . (Romans 8:28)

SS20024

We Must Believe

Do you have a hard time believing in God? According to the Bible, it is quite a simple formula. The hard part is doing what God wants us to do all of the time. Find the words from the Bible verse in the word search. Look up, down, forward, backward, and diagonally. Then write the verse on the lines below.

```
J E S U S I S L O R D I
Y D A E D M I H H R G W
R S V P Y B L T X P Z I
U U E A J O U T H A T L
O B D N S O U U D A Y L
Y H E D M U J R O P T B
N R T L D T E V P Y Q E
I A U I I H I O V B F S
J I O Z W E F D O G J I
X S Y E R R V T R A E H
G E A Y O X T E U F R W
Q D K M K C O N F E S S
```

THAT	WITH	JESUS IS LORD	IN YOUR	GOD	FROM	YOU
IF YOU	YOUR	AND	HEART	RAISED	THE	WILL BE
CONFESS	MOUTH	BELIEVE	THAT	HIM	DEAD	SAVED

_____ _____ _____ _____

_____ _____, "_____ ___ __ _____,"

_____ _____ _____ _____

_____ _____ _____ _____.

_____ _____, _____ _____

(Romans 10:9)

SS20024

Love Is . . .

In the Bible, we are told a lot about the love of God. What is love? How does love act? Write the words of the verse on the lines below as they appear on the heart. Cut the heart on the bold lines, mix up the pieces, and put the heart together. Say the verse again.

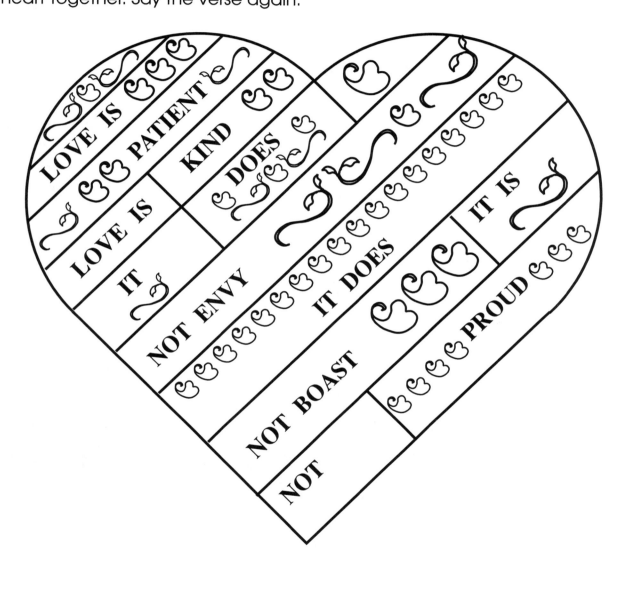

_____

_____

_____ (1 Corinthians 13:4)

SS20024

New Life in Christ

When we find Christ and accept Him as our Savior, we are a new person in God's eyes. Learn more about this by filling in the correct consonant in each blank.

__ __E__E__O__E, I__ A__ __O__E I__ I__

__ __ __I__ __, __E I__ A __E__ __ __EA__IO__;

__ __E O__ __ __A__ __O__E, __ __E __E__

__A__ __O__E!

Write the verse.

_____

_____

_____ (2 Corinthians 5:17)

SS20024

Crucified With Christ

The Bible tells us that Christ died for us. He wants us to live for Him. Did you know that if we are crucified with Christ, we will live again? Use the code to find a relating verse. Write the verse below.

```
 9      8  1  22  5      2  5  5  14
___    __ _  __  _      _  _  _  __

 3  18  21  3   9  6  9  5  4
__  __  __  _   _  _  _  _  _

23  9  20  8      3  8  18  9  19  20
__  _  __  _      _  _  __  _  __  __

 1  14  4      9      14  15      12  15  14  7  5  18
_   __  _      _      __  __      __  __  __  _  _  __

12  9  22  5 ,     2  21  20      3  8  18  9  19  20
__  _  __  _       _  __  __      _  _  __  _  __  __

12  9  22  5  19      9  14      13  5  . . .    (Galatians 2:20)
__  _  __  _  __      _  __      __  _
```

Fruit of the Spirit

In the Bible, we read about the fruits of the Spirit. Many know that love is one of these fruits. To learn about other fruits of the Spirit, write a special verse on the lines below. To do this, write the first word in section 1 and continue by writing the first word in sections 2 through 4. Then write the second word in section 1 and continue until all the words in each section have been written.

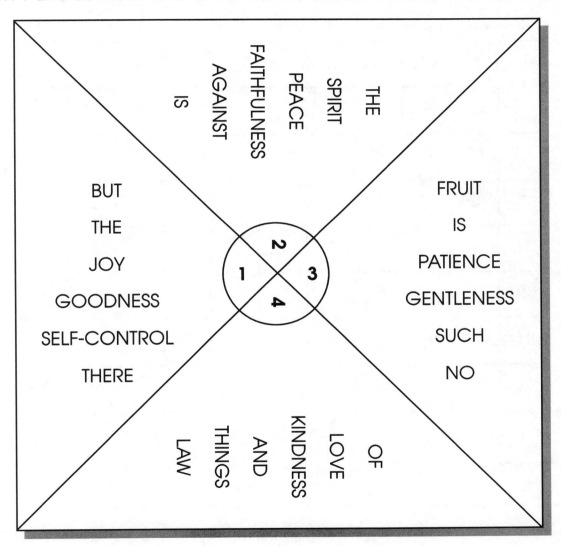

_____

_____

_____

_____ (Galatians 5:22–23)

SS20024

Gift of God

We cannot earn God's pleasure. His great love for us is a free gift. To find out more about this gift of God, write every letter in the odd columns starting with **F** and going across. Then go back and write all the letters in the even columns starting with **T**.

1	2	3	4	5	6	7	8	9	10	11
F	T	O	H	R	I	I	S	T	N	I
S	O	B	T	Y	F	G	R	R	O	A
C	M	E	Y	Y	O	O	U	U	R	H
A	S	V	E	E	L	B	V	E	E	E
N	S	S	I	A	T	V	I	E	S	D
T	T	H	H	R	E	O	G	U	I	G
H	F	F	T	A	O	I	F	T	G	H
A	O	N	D	D						

Write the verse.

F _____

_____

T _____

_____

_____ (Ephesians 2:8)

50

SS20024

Rejoice

Be happy in the Lord. The Bible tells us to rejoice in Christ. If we love Jesus, we will rejoice in our hearts and with our lips. Fit the words from the Bible verse below into the puzzle. One word has been done for you. Several letters have also been provided. Write the verse on the lines under the boxes.

REJOICE	WILL	I	SAY	THE	ALWAYS
LORD	AGAIN	IN	REJOICE	IT	

REJOICE _____

_____

_____ (Philippians 4:4)

SS20024

Strength in Christ

Do you know someone who is very strong? There are different kinds of strength. Fit the underlined words into the squares to learn how you can grow strong. Then write the verse on the lines.

I <u>CAN</u> DO <u>EVERYTHING</u> <u>THROUGH</u> <u>HIM</u> <u>WHO</u> <u>GIVES</u> <u>ME</u> <u>STRENGTH.</u>

(Philippians 4:13)

Write the verse.

_____

_____

_____

SS20024

God Meets Our Needs

We need very few things to actually survive on this planet. However, we may want many things. According to God's Word, our needs and our wants are very different.

Unscramble the words on the left and write them on the lines to find out how God supplies our needs.

DAN   _____

YM   _____

ODG   _____

LIWL   _____

TEME   _____

LAL   _____

RUYO   _____

DENSE   _____

CADNCROGI   _____

OT   _____

ISH   _____

ROIGUSLO   _____

CERSIH   _____

NI   _____

STHRCI   _____

SJSEU   _____

Write the verse.

_____

_____

_____ (Philippians 4:19)

SS20024

Thankful

Can you think of someone you are thankful for? Have you told this person that you are thankful for him or her? To find out a verse about being thankful, decode the verse using the key below.

1–H	4–U	7–W	10–P	13–C	16–T	19–M	22–Z	25–N
2–O	5–K	8–J	11–D	14–I	17–B	20–A	23–G	26–F
3–R	6–Y	9–E	12–Q	15–L	18–V	21–X	24–S	

$\overline{7}\ \overline{9}$ $\overline{20}\ \overline{15}\ \overline{7}\ \overline{20}\ \overline{6}\ \overline{24}$ $\overline{16}\ \overline{1}\ \overline{20}\ \overline{25}\ \overline{5}$

$\overline{23}\ \overline{2}\ \overline{11}$ $\overline{26}\ \overline{2}\ \overline{3}$ $\overline{20}\ \overline{15}\ \overline{15}$ $\overline{2}\ \overline{26}$

$\overline{6}\ \overline{2}\ \overline{4}$, $\overline{19}\ \overline{9}\ \overline{25}\ \overline{16}\ \overline{14}\ \overline{2}\ \overline{25}\ \overline{14}\ \overline{25}\ \overline{23}$

$\overline{6}\ \overline{2}\ \overline{4}$ $\overline{14}\ \overline{25}$ $\overline{2}\ \overline{4}\ \overline{3}$

$\overline{10}\ \overline{3}\ \overline{20}\ \overline{6}\ \overline{9}\ \overline{3}\ \overline{24}$. (1 Thessalonians 1:2)

SS20024

Morse Code

What is faith? We cannot see it or touch it, but we know it is there. We can see the results of faith when we believe in God. Use the Morse code below to find a verse relating to faith.

A ▪—	G ▬▬▪	M ▬▬	S ▪▪▪	Y ▬▪▬▬
B ▬▪▪▪	H ▪▪▪▪	N ▬▪	T ▬	Z ▬▬▪▪
C ▬▪▬▪	I ▪▪	O ▬▬▬	U ▪▪▬	
D ▬▪▪	J ▪▬▬▬	P ▪▬▬▪	V ▪▪▪▬	
E ▪	K ▬▪▬	Q ▬▬▪▬	W ▪▬▬	
F ▪▪▬▪	L ▪▬▪▪	R ▪▬▪	X ▬▪▪▬	

(Hebrews 11:1)

© Shining Star Publications

SS20024

Always the Same

The Bible is God's Word, and it will never change. Heaven and earth may pass away, but God's Word will remain the same. A related verse tells us about this God who is always the same. Follow the directions carefully to find out the verse.

Cross out the number words in lines 2, 5, and 10.
Cross out the animal names in lines 1, 3, 6, 8, and 9.
Cross out the color words in lines 2, 4, 5, 6, 8, and 10.
Cross out the girls' names in lines 1, 4, 7, and 9.
Cross out all the "X's" in lines 7, 8, and 9.
Cross out the boys' names in lines 3, 7, and 9.
Cross out the last two letters in lines 4 and 7.
Cross out the last letter in lines 5, 8, and 9.

1. JESUSCAROLHORSE
2. TWOPURPLECHRIST
3. ISDAVIDELEPHANT
4. RUTHTHEBROWNOI
5. TWENTYBLACKSAMEE
6. ANTYESTERDAYRED
7. XANDJOYCEJOHNTO
8. COWXTODAYWHITET
9. XBEARBOBSUEANDA
10. FOURBLUEFOREVER

Write the remaining words for the verse.

_____

_____

_____ (Hebrews 13:8)

SS20024

Crown of Glory

The Bible speaks of different kinds of crowns. If we are faithful to Jesus here on earth, we will be crowned with glory. Start with the word **And** in the top half of the crown and then go to the first word under the thick line on the bottom part of the crown. Write these words. Then go back and forth until you find a complete verse about a crown.

AND   THE   SHEPHERD   YOU

RECEIVE   CROWN   GLORY   WILL   FADE

WHEN   CHIEF   APPEARS,   WILL

THE   OF   THAT   NEVER   AWAY

(1 PETER 5:4)

Write the words for the verse.

_____

_____

_____ (1 Peter 5:4)

SS20024

God Cares for Us

Many times in the Bible, we are told how God cares for us. Use the keypad to find out how much He cares for us. The first number tells you what key to look at. The second number tells you which letter to write.

Example: 3–1 = D

___ ___ ___ ___ ___ ___ ___ ___ ___ ___ ___
2–3 2–1 7–3 8–1 2–1 5–3 5–3 9–3 6–3 8–2 7–2

___ ___ ___ ___ ___ ___ ___ ___ ___ ___ ___ ___
2–1 6–2 9–2 4–3 3–2 8–1 9–3 6–3 6–2 4–2 4–3 6–1

___ ___ ___ ___ ___ ___ ___ ___ ___
2–2 3–2 2–3 2–1 8–2 7–3 3–2 4–2 3–2

___ ___ ___ ___ ___ ___ ___ ___ ___ ___ ___.
2–3 2–1 7–2 3–2 7–3 3–3 6–3 7–2 9–3 6–3 8–2

(1 Peter 5:7)

SS20024

Pleased

God gave His one and only Son to the world. Jesus gave His life for us. He did this because He loves us very much. Today, we can live for Him who died for us. Each letter below stands for the letter in the alphabet that comes after it. (Use A after Z.) The first letter is done for you.

Tip: Write each word of the verse on a piece of paper, mixed-up. Then without looking, try to put it in the right order by numbering each word.

. . . "T___ ___ ___ ___,
   S   G H R   H R   L X   R N M

___ ___ ___ ___; ___
V G N L   H   K N U D   V H S G

___ ___ ___ ___
G H L   H   Z L   V D K K

___." (2 Peter 1:17)
O K D Z R D C

Write the verse using correct punctuation.

_____

_____

_____

    SS20024

God Is Love

Throughout the Bible, we are told of God's love for us. He loves us now, and His love for us is everlasting. God cares for you. He loves you. No matter what may happen to you, or wherever you may go, God's love is always with you.

Unscramble the letters below. Then write the words on the blank lines.

HIST　　　　　_____

SI　　　　　　_____

VOLE:　　　 _____

ONT　　　　　_____

HTTA　　　　_____

EW　　　　　 _____

DVLEO　　　 _____

DGO,　　　　_____

BTU　　　　　_____

ATHT　　　　_____

EH　　　　　 _____

DOVEL　　　 _____

SU . . .　　 _____

Write the verse.

_____

_____

_____ (1 John 4:10)

　　　　　　　　　　　　　　　　　　SS20024

Answer Key

Page 4

In the beginning God created the heavens and the earth.

Page 5

So God created man in his own image, in the image of God he created him; male and female he created them.

Page 6

"Honor your father and your mother, so that you may live long in the land the Lord your God is giving you."

Page 7

Love the Lord your God with all your heart and with all your soul and with all your strength.

Page 8

"The eternal God is your refuge, and underneath are the everlasting arms . . ."

Page 9

"Now fear the Lord and serve him with all faithfulness . . ."

Page 10

Give thanks to the Lord, for he is good; his love endures forever.

Page 11

O Lord, our Lord, how majestic is your name in all the earth! . . .

Page 12

The precepts of the Lord are right, giving joy to the heart . . .

Page 13

Surely goodness and love will follow me all the days of my life, and I will dwell in the house of the Lord forever.

Page 14

The earth is the Lord's, and everything in it, the world, and all who live in it.

Page 15

Create in me a pure heart, O God, and renew a steadfast spirit within me.

Page 16

They rejoice in your name all day long; they exult in your righteousness.

Page 17

The Lord is compassionate and gracious, slow to anger, abounding in love.

Page 18

This is the day the Lord has made; let us rejoice and be glad in it.

Page 19

I have hidden your word in my heart that I might not sin against you. (Psalm 119:11)

Page 20

Your word is a lamp to my feet and a light for my path.

Page 21

The Lord reigns forever, your God, O Zion, for all generations.

Page 22

Trust in the Lord with all your heart and lean not on your own understanding; in all your ways acknowledge him, and he will make your paths straight.

Page 23

. . . "Holy, holy, holy is the Lord Almighty; the whole earth is full of his glory."

Page 24

So do not fear, for I am with you; do not be dismayed, for I am your God. I will strengthen you and help you . . .

Page 25

When your words came, I ate them; they were my joy and my heart's delight . . .

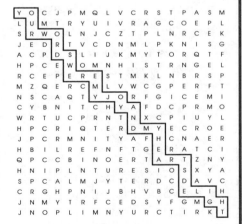

SS20024

Answer Key

Page 26

. . . "I have loved you with an everlasting love; I have drawn you with loving-kindness."

Page 27

The Lord is good, a refuge in times of trouble. He cares for those who trust in him.

Page 28

"The virgin will be with child and will give birth to a son, and they will call him Immanuel"—which means, "God with us."

Page 29

"Come, follow me," Jesus said, "and I will make you fishers of men."

Page 30

"Blessed are the pure in heart, for they will see God."

Page 31

"In the same way, let your light shine before men, that they may see your good deeds and praise your Father in heaven."

Page 32

". . . Love your enemies and pray for those who persecute you."

Page 33

"Ask and it will be given to you; seek and you will find; knock and the door will be opened to you."

Page 34

Then he touched their eyes and said, "According to your faith will it be done to you."

Page 35

And this was his message: "After me will come one more powerful than I, the thongs of whose sandals I am not worthy to stoop down and untie."

Page 36

"Whoever welcomes one of these little children in my name welcomes me . . ."

Page 37

. . . "What is impossible with men is possible with God."

Page 38

"For God so loved the world that he gave his one and only Son, that whoever believes in him shall not perish but have eternal life."

Page 39

Jesus answered, "I am the way and the truth and the life. No one comes to the Father except through me."

Page 40

"'And everyone who calls on the name of the Lord will be saved.'"

Page 41

They replied, "Believe in the Lord Jesus, and you will be saved—you and your household."

Page 42

But God demonstrates his own love for us in this: While we were still sinners, Christ died for us.

Page 43

For the wages of sin is death, but the gift of God is eternal life in Christ Jesus our Lord.

Page 44

And we know that in all things God works for the good of those who love him . . .

Page 45

That if you confess with your mouth, "Jesus is Lord," and believe in your heart that God raised him from the dead, you will be saved.

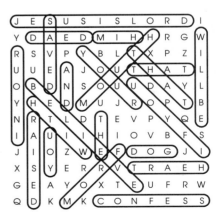

SS20024

Answer Key

Page 46

Love is patient, love is kind. It does not envy, it does not boast, it is not proud.

Page 47

Therefore, if anyone is in Christ, he is a new creation; the old has gone, the new has come!

Page 48

I have been crucified with Christ and I no longer live, but Christ lives in me . . .

Page 49

But the fruit of the Spirit is love, joy, peace, patience, kindness, goodness, faithfulness, gentleness and self-control. Against such things there is no law.

Page 50

For it is by grace you have been saved, through faith—and this not from yourselves, it is the gift of God.

Page 51

Rejoice in the Lord always. I will say it again: Rejoice!

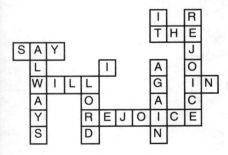

Page 52

I can do everything through him who gives me strength.

Page 53

And my God will meet all your needs according to his glorious riches in Christ Jesus.

Page 54

We always thank God for all of you, mentioning you in our prayers.

Page 55

Now faith is being sure of what we hope for and certain of what we do not see.

Page 56

Jesus Christ is the same yesterday and today and forever.

Page 57

And when the Chief Shepherd appears, you will receive the crown of glory that will never fade away.

Page 58

Cast all your anxiety on him because he cares for you.

Page 59

. . . "This is my Son, whom I love; with him I am well pleased."

Page 60

This is love: not that we loved God, but that he loved us . . .

© Shining Star Publications
63
SS20024

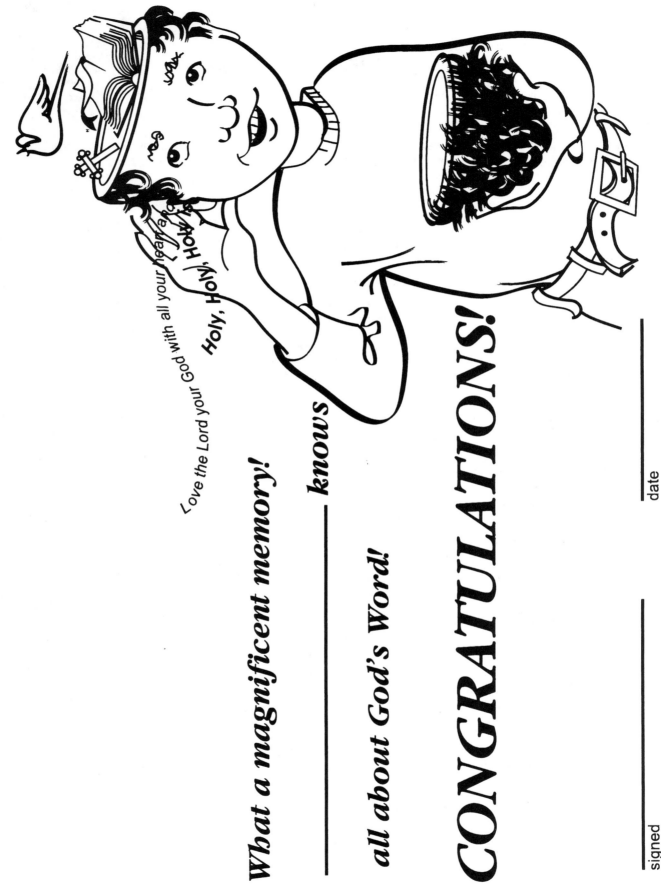

Love the Lord your God with all your heart...

Holy, Holy, Holy...

What a magnificent memory!

_____ knows

all about God's Word!

CONGRATULATIONS!

_____ signed

_____ date

SS20024